MY BROTHER'S KEEPER

THE HOLOCAUST THROUGH
THE EYES OF AN ARTIST

ISRAEL BERNBAUM

G.P. PUTNAM'S SONS   New York

Copyright © 1985 by Israel Bernbaum
All rights reserved. Published simultaneously
in Canada by General Publishing Co. Limited, Toronto.
Printed in the United States of America.
First impression
Designed by Nanette Stevenson

Library of Congress Cataloging in Publication Data
Bernbaum, Israel.   My brother's keeper.
Bibliography: p.
Summary: The author describes the Holocaust and
explains how he tries to tell the story of that
catastrophic slaughter of Jews through his art.
1. Bernbaum, Israel—Juvenile literature.
2. Holocaust, Jewish (1939-1945), in art—Juvenile
literature. [1. Holocaust, Jewish (1939-1945), in
art. 2. Holocaust, Jewish (1939-1945)] I. Title.
ND237.B53A4 1985   759.13   84-16100
ISBN 0-399-21242-6

Quotation on page 6 taken from the edition of the Bible published by
The Soncino Press, London, Jerusalem, New York. 1979.

Israel Bernbaum's paintings were photographed for this book by Richard Benson.

Every effort has been made to trace the ownership of all copyrighted material.
In the event of any question arising as to the use of any material, the author
and the publisher, while expressing regret for any inadvertent error, will be happy
to make the necessary correction in future printings.

My paintings are dedicated to the memory
of the one and a half million Jewish children who
did not survive the Holocaust.

This book is dedicated to my children David,
Aviezer, and Zvi, to the Jewish children
who miraculously survived the Holocaust, and to
the children of survivors.

My paintings and this book are also dedicated to
all the children on our planet with my ardent
wish that they live in security in a world of love,
brotherhood, and peace.

ACKNOWLEDGMENTS

This book presents my paintings of the greatest tragedy in human history, the Holocaust. I have been able to create my paintings only because in 1957 this blessed country of ours granted me a homeland, freedom, and gates wide open to opportunities and education. It is most appropriate that my first words of acknowledgment and deep gratitude are to the people of the United States of America.

I would like to express my most ardent words of gratitude to my Editor Refna Wilkin and Art Director Nanette Stevenson, who devoted all their expertise, talent, and dedication toward making this book appear in this splendid form.

My sincere thanks go to author Judy Blume for her kind interest and advice.

I feel most indebted to my alma mater, Queens College of the City University of New York, where in 1973 I received a Bachelor of Arts degree with a major in Fine Arts, cum laude. My special gratitude to my Professors of Art Charles F. Cajori, Elias S. Friedensohn, Gerald Hahn, and Harry Kramer for their interest and support in my Holocaust work and for their guidance.

I owe a special debt of gratitude to Mr. Herman Bogdan, Principal of Public School 173, Fresh Meadow, Queens, New York, and his teachers. Over a number of years, they gave me the unique opportunity to bring the story of the Holocaust to all the children of the school through my art. The endless class discussions and the hundreds of letters that I received from the children were an inspiring factor in the conception of this book.

My words of gratitude go to Dr. Azriel Eisenberg, leading scholar and author of monumental books on the Holocaust, for his encouraging words of recognition for my art. Most valuable were his kind suggestions and corrections after reading my manuscript.

I would like to thank Susan Rachlin and Art Director Temima Gezari of the Board of Jewish Education of Greater New York for exhibiting my paintings in the children's gallery.

My appreciation to Judith Muffs of the Anti-Defamation League of B'nai B'rith District #1 for reading the manuscript and for her valuable remarks.

I wish to express my gratitude to the President Jack Eisner and Director Shirley Eisner-Gibson of the Holocaust Survivors Memorial Foundation for their helping hand in time of need.

CONTENTS

. . . *Cain rose up against his brother and slew him.*

   And the Lord said unto Cain: "Where is Abel thy brother?" And he said: "I know not; am I my brother's keeper?" And He said: "What hast thou done? The voice of thy brother's blood crieth unto Me from the ground."

Genesis IV, 8

REMEMBER

I tell the story of the Holocaust through art. Lines, shapes and colors are my language. The language of art can leave a more lasting impression than words and has a universal appeal. I want to talk through my paintings to all the people of the world. The story of the Holocaust must be of concern to everyone. Six million Jews died, among them one and a half million children. Who killed them? Who were the people who kept silent while they watched the slaughter? What happened to humanity and to our civilization?

There is no limit to the questions we can ask about the Holocaust, but to one question we must find an answer: How can we prevent it from happening again?

In our democratic society, in the United States, the future lies in the hands of the people. We can build a stable future only by knowing the past. It is my hope that my paintings and this book will help you to avoid the mistakes of the past in order to build a glorious future for all people.

I sincerely hope that you will like my art and learn an important lesson from it: To be your brother's keeper.

What was the Holocaust? What was unique about the Holocaust? you may ask.

During World War II about fifty million people lost their lives. However, proportionally, the Jewish people suffered the most catastrophic losses. Two out of three Jewish people in Europe were killed in a mass slaughter of an extent never before known in human history. That was done according to a plan that was prepared and organized by the German government under the dictatorship of Adolf Hitler. Its aim was the extermination of the total Jewish population of the world.

This mass murder historians call the "Holocaust." "Holocaust" means a fire totally consuming a sacrificial victim, according to ancient practice. It is a fire engulfing any living being in its path. The fires of Hitler's Holocaust engulfed the lives of six million Jewish men, women and children.

Hitler and his German Nazi Party prepared a list of eleven million Jews to be killed. To accomplish this incredible crime on such an immense scale, the Germans built a great number of slave labor camps and death camps all over Europe. They organized a special system of cattle trains which delivered the Jewish victims to their deaths.

To us, citizens of the United States, it sounds unbelievable. Just because the unbelievable really took place, and it happened in recent times, and in the most cultured and civilized countries in Europe, we may ask: What was wrong with the people that they let it happen? Would Americans allow such a tragedy as the Holocaust?

To find answers to these questions it is important to look at how events developed in Germany, the country that masterminded the Holocaust.

In 1918, after World War I, Germany became a republic with a democratic form of government. There was a parliament with free elections and parties with different political programs. In 1920, Adolf Hitler with his Nazi Party (National Socialist German Workers' Party) appeared with new political ideas.

Hitler differed from all other political leaders because of his relentless anti-Semitic propaganda, accusing the Jews of all the evil that happened in Germany and in the world. The Jewish people could not do much to defend themselves because they were a tiny minority. They represented only one percent of the total population of Germany.

Hitler was a cunning and ambitious politician. He knew how to use the old religious hostility against the Jews to his favor in his struggle for political power. In his violent speeches he held the Jews responsible for Germany's losing the World War in 1918. The Jews, who had lived in Germany for many generations, loved their country. They were very patriotic and fought in German wars, often receiving medals for bravery. This did not prevent Hitler from attacking the Jews with lies and false accusations.

In addition to preaching anti-Semitism, Hitler claimed that Germans were superior to all other peoples, and that Nature had made them the master race. All the rest of the people, Hitler stated, were fit only to be their slaves. At the time many Germans were delighted by these racial theories and took them seriously.

Hitler promised that Germany would become the greatest empire in the world, which would last for one thousand years. The Germans believed him, and in 1933, Hitler was elected the Chancellor of Germany. With the help of hundreds of thousands of Nazi storm troopers, Hitler seized unlimited power as dictator and the Germans obeyed him blindly.

After careful preparations, Hitler launched his great armies against my country, Poland. I vividly remember that, on September 1, 1939, we were awakened at five in the morning by blasts from bombs dropped during heavy air raids. In a few hours, our whole country was in flames. September 1, 1939, was the first day of World War II, which lasted until 1945.

At the beginning, the German armies were very successful. Their troops occupied many of the countries in Europe. Wherever the Germans appeared with their troops, they brought destruction, suffering, torture and death to millions.

The people of the United States realized that Hitler's Germany presented a great danger to the security of their country and to the world. Under the presidency of Franklin Delano Roosevelt, they joined Great Britain and the Soviet Union in a long difficult war against Nazi Germany.

Ultimately, Germany was defeated, and in 1945, Hitler killed himself in his bunker in Berlin. Many Nazi leaders were captured. They were tried by an International Military Tribunal, and all were convicted of crimes against humanity. They were sentenced to be hanged or to serve long prison terms. Through great efforts and many sacrifices, the people of Europe with the Soviet Union and the United States put an end to the domination of Nazi Germany.

When the war ended, the whole continent of Europe, from the French shores of the Atlantic to the gates of Moscow, had suffered terrible destruction. Close to fifty million people lost their lives, including civilians of bombed cities in Europe, but the heaviest price was paid by the Jewish people because they were innocent victims of the Holocaust.

There are thousands of books written by Holocaust survivors, those who miraculously escaped death from the hands of the German S.S. (The S.S. was Hitler's Elite Guard, a special police force, which also operated in concentration camps and death camps.) There are also many books written by scholars and historians who not only describe events that took place, but also try to find some explanations. There are films and television shows that try to revive the tragic past of the Holocaust.

I, however, have tried to revive the Holocaust in my large paintings—in bold, sharp colors, heavy lines, and through various arrangements of figures and shapes. By creating these paintings, I wished to attract your attention, to evoke your interest. I wanted to move your hearts, and to stimulate your thinking and your wish to learn.

You can easily understand that when I created my paintings I was deeply moved emotionally. After the war, when I returned to my homeland, Poland, I found my world, in which I had lived and which had been so dear to me, completely in ashes. The deserted ruins and the mountains of rubble were the result not of war but of the Holocaust.

If I hadn't escaped in time from Warsaw my destiny would not have been different from those of the six million Jews. I was already on the Germans' registration list. Most likely the Gestapo (the German secret police), was looking for me. From my once large family I was one of the few survivors.

The series of my paintings on the Holocaust I call "Warsaw Ghetto 1943."

You will ask why "Warsaw" and why "1943"? Warsaw, the capital of Poland, is the city of my birth. I embrace it in my memory as I remember it. I grew up there, with my dreams and expectations, in the spiritually rich, exciting, and vibrant Jewish world that had existed in Poland for a thousand years. Three hundred and fifty thousand Jews were living there. It was considered the spiritual center of world Jewry. The year 1943 entered history as the year that marked the destruction of Jewish life in Warsaw. Its end symbolized the end of Jewish existence in Europe under Nazi Germany.

Each painting in the series, according to its title, is on a different topic. Each varies in its structure and details. They form "chapters" of one "book." The book is the Holocaust. When you look at the paintings, you see red as the predominant color. I could not help but see the world of the Ghetto symbolically soaked in blood, buried in bricks from the ruins, walls piled over walls, and raging with flames. On the other sides of the walls you will find contrasting colors. You'll see greenery, blue skies, flowers in pots and smiling people.

My paintings should not be interpreted as illustrations of specific events. I am using symbolic figures, symbolic colors and symbolic situations. I have tried to transfer to my paintings my feelings, my anxieties, and my revulsion against a world of injustice and brutality. I wish my paintings could shout words of accusation and condemnation. However, I am fully aware that no words, no speech, nor any form of art, or any human expression will be able to tell the whole story of the Holocaust. Therefore, as much as it is humanly possible to tell this story, it must be told. My paintings are only a modest contribution to the moral obligation of telling about the Holocaust. It must be done for the sake of the children of today, for future generations and in remembrance of so many innocent victims.

I am also fulfilling my duty to tell the story of the Holocaust by presenting my paintings in public and in high schools through slides. I treasure most the several hundred letters which I received from pupils commenting on my art and the Holocaust. These letters show how students, after learning about the tragic events, are anxious to know how to prevent such a disaster from happening again.

THE WARSAW GHETTO STREETS 1943

Oil on canvas, 60" × 90" (152 cm. × 228.6 cm.), 1979

You don't see real streets in this painting. There are no buildings here. You see some ruins of buildings and pieces of rubble inscribed with names of streets which existed at one time. *Ulica (oolitza)* in Polish means "street." Each street in Warsaw, and in the Jewish section as well, had tall buildings with large balconies. The streets were usually very crowded with lively traffic.

The Polish people were proud of their capital, Warsaw, with its one million inhabitants. One-third of the people were Jews, who had lived there for many centuries.

After the invasion of Warsaw the Germans started to carry out their plan for killing the Jews. Their first step was a strict order to register the whole Jewish population. Then, the German authorities issued instructions for moving all the Jews into a restricted area of the Jewish section.

In 1940 an order was given to erect a tall, thick wall around the streets designated for the Jews to live. This became known as the Warsaw Ghetto Wall. The Jews had to confine themselves by building the wall and were compelled to pay for its expenses. The

THE WARSAW GHETTO

Germans' purpose was to seal off the Jews from the rest of the world, to humiliate them, starve them, and then to deport every single man, woman and child to die in the death camps. The Germans used the same system in every city in Poland where Jews lived in large numbers.

After the Ghetto was established in Warsaw, the Germans moved over 500,000 Jews into this area where before the war 80,000 had lived. In 1942, the

Germans started mass deportation of the Ghetto population to the death camps. For over a year, day after day, with small interruptions, loads of cattle trains with men, women and children left the specially built train station in Warsaw for Treblinka, the notorious death camp.

In April 1943, the Germans decided to completely liquidate the Warsaw Ghetto. According to their plan, the more than 50,000 Jews still remaining had to be deported in two or three days. German General Jürgen Stroop was in charge of carrying out this plan. The Jewish young people rose in revolt against the Germans. This event became known in history as the Warsaw Ghetto Uprising. The heroic Jewish rebels fought the mighty German army for five weeks. In revenge, General Stroop completely demolished the Ghetto with fire, dynamite and gas. On May 16, 1943, he reported to his superior that "There is no longer a Jewish quarter in Warsaw." He used this short sentence in his diary of his military actions, accompanied by photographs of the Warsaw ruins and of captured Jewish rebels. The diary is known as "General Stroop's Report."

In order to make my paintings historically truthful, many images are based on photographs taken by German soldiers. The photographs in General Stroop's Report were a source of many images in my paintings. The very idea of creating *The Warsaw Ghetto Streets 1943* came to me from one of the German photographs, which especially shocked me when I saw it for the first time: It shows a view of ruins and rubble in an area where once a street was located. In front, on a pile of crushed walls, can be seen one fragment with an inscription on it, "Ulica Karmelicka."

Karmelicka Street was especially close to my heart. My grandparents had lived there, and so had many members of my large family and many friends. It was one of the more elegant streets in Warsaw, with beautiful stores, movie houses, synagogues and Jewish institutions.

The photograph shows what happened to Karmelicka Street. At the same time it gives us an idea what happened to the street where I had lived, Muranowska Street, and to the many other Warsaw streets where my people lived for centuries. All the street names have disappeared along with the buildings. I created my paintings so that their previous existence will not disappear from our memory. These names were intimately interwoven with the life and history of the Jewish people of Warsaw. When people who once lived in Warsaw see my painting for the first time, many of them search for the street in which they had lived.

A photograph from Stroop's Report shows a street in the burning Ghetto with a corner building enveloped in flames and smoke. I recognized on its wall the street sign with the name Ulica Gesia. Before the war, Gesia Street was a world center of the textile industry. My painting includes the ruins of the building, with the street sign "Ulica Gesia."

Balconies were part of the Warsaw landscape. Almost all apartments, including ours, had their balconies, where you could relax and see your neighbors. Two yards away from our balcony, a blue, slender electric pole, with its two iron arms, was holding the high-tension wires servicing the electric streetcars.

In my painting, the blue electric pole is broken. It is leaning over a balcony which is about to fall. I show the two objects—the balcony and the electric

pole—with which the memories of my childhood and youth are linked, in their final stage of existence, as if they are weeping together over the fate of the people whom they had served silently and faithfully for so many years.

The one-thousand-year-old culture of Jewish creativity in Poland was destroyed and an attempt was made to erase all traces of its existence. I symbolized this destruction by the burning scrolls, books and papers. The Jews' love for music is represented by the broken violin. Next to this image we see the ruins of the Warsaw Synagogue.

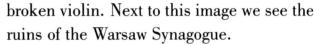

There is a photograph showing the blown-up Warsaw Great Synagogue, which was also called Tlomackie Synagogue, because it was on Tlomackie Street. In my painting I show the collapsed building with a broken Holy Ark, a shattered stained-glass window from the Synagogue, and skeletons of once beautiful menorahs.

The Warsaw Great Synagogue and the adjacent building of the world-famous Judaica Library survived undamaged despite heavy bombing during the first German assault on Warsaw in September 1939. When the Ghetto Wall was built, the Germans left the Synagogue outside the Ghetto. They desecrated it by using it as a warehouse for the furniture which had been taken away from the Jews of the Ghetto. After the destruction of the Warsaw Ghetto, the Synagogue building still stood undamaged.

To mark the final victory of the mighty German army over the defenseless remnants of the Jewish civilians of the Ghetto, the Germans chose to blow up the Warsaw Great Synagogue with its library. By this act of vandalism they also wanted to prove their victory over the Jewish spiritual heritage.

The ruins of the Warsaw Great Synagogue in my painting may serve as a memorial to its glory and as a reminder of what happens when hatred and prejudice dominate the world. The beautiful house of worship on Tlomackie Street in Warsaw vanished together with its worshipers as victims of the Holocaust.

The Germans could never succeed in destroying what the Synagogue stood for—the Jewish faith and the Jewish spirit. This indestructible nature of the Jewish faith is symbolized by the figure enveloped in the prayer shawl (tallith) firmly holding a Torah (holy scroll), the first five books of the Hebrew Bible. This figure emerges like the legendary phoenix, renewed from the ashes and flames of burning books and scrolls.

The Torah, in the hands of the figure, symbolizes the ultimate triumph of human values and human spirit over the evil of racism, prejudice and hatred. The Torah, the Bible, contains the oldest divine message to humanity.

Photographs of the destroyed Warsaw Great Synagogue show skeletons of menorahs. In my painting you can

recognize the menorahs placed in different parts. The few Jewish survivors who witnessed the deafening blast of the blown-up Synagogue were amazed to find the skeletons of the menorahs standing unbroken, upright. They took it as a prophetic sign that light would prevail over the darkness of barbarism. In Jewish tradition, a menorah symbolizes spiritual light. In my painting, they are standing over the ruins of the Ghetto like two light-bearing guardians.

You see the walls of the Ghetto embracing its deserted ruins. The last residents, before they were dragged away on their final journey by German S.S. men, left on walls their desperate appeal written in Yiddish: *"GEDENK"*— REMEMBER. Yiddish was the language of the Jewish people in Eastern Europe. The message REMEMBER in my painting is addressed to all people and nations.

Let us look at what is going on on the other side of the walls, on the so-called Aryan side. According to the Nazi racial theory, an Aryan is a non-Jew of Caucasian stock—and therefore racially "pure." There we see greenery, clean, colorful buildings with flowers on their balconies. Street lamps are ready to provide light, symbolizing that life is flowing undisrupted. The triumphant Nazi flags stand proudly on rooftops.

When we look at the lower left-hand corner of the painting, we notice another Nazi flag, but symbolically it is being trampled upon

by a Ghetto resistance fighter. The young Jewish hero defying the German enemy is raising high a flag of Zion, the flag of hope and survival. The heroic young fighters emerge from the underground announcing by their presence that the fight for Jewish existence will continue. The figures of the two young women fighters are from Stroop's Report. I pay tribute to them, as well as to all who perished in the Ghetto uprising.

On the flag of Zion held by the hero is a slogan written with blood in Hebrew: *"Am Israel Chai,"* which means "Long Live the Jewish People." The hero is holding the flag with confidence and pride.

ON BOTH SIDES OF THE WARSAW GHETTO WALL

Oil on canvas, 40″ × 60″ (101.6 cm. × 152.4 cm.), 1973

As you can tell from the title of this painting, my concern was with presenting not only what was taking place inside the Ghetto but also what was going on outside its walls.

From the previous painting you know what the Germans had done to the Jews. But you may wonder, how did the Christian world act in view of this Jewish tragedy? You may ask, what did the Polish people do? Did they help their Jewish neighbors with whom they shared a one-thousand-year history?

From the first glance at my painting, you can see that the Jews were totally isolated and surrounded by a hostile world. In many instances non-Jewish people helped the Germans against their Jewish neighbors. There were, however, exceptions.

The Ghetto walls formed a sealed unit with a few heavily guarded gates. No one could move in or out without permission. Violators were arrested or shot on the spot. In this painting, the wall is open to show what is happening at the same time on both sides.

What you see here is symbolic. The images present only ideas,

not actual events. They tell in general terms how it was. For example, when I show the huge clown, I want only to say that, when the Ghetto was burning, the people on the other side were having a good time and laughing. A clown is a symbol of fun.

However, in order to make my paintings historically accurate, I based many images on photographs taken by German soldiers. Many of those who appeared on our streets had cameras and were taking pictures during their attacks on their Jewish victims.

In the photograph on the left, we see a street enveloped in smoke and flames. Armed soldiers are in action. From the upper floor a man is falling to his death. This illustrates one of many similar events which took place during the liquidation of the Ghetto.

In the photograph on the right, we see people lying on the ground. One victim was picked up to be included in the picture. To ridicule him, the Germans ordered him to put on a prayer shawl. The soldiers behind him had a good laugh. This photograph is indeed a document of human cruelty.

Another picture demonstrating human brutality is this one showing women and children with raised hands. Especially striking is the little boy with the frightened face, his hands above his head. The soldier behind him is posing with a smile for the camera while he aims his machine gun at the child. You can see that the situations seen in my paintings are not just the imagination of an artist.

In this painting, let us look first inside the Ghetto. We see the front of a building in flames. Jewish people are trapped in their apartments and balconies. A mother with two children is praying to God. A man in a prayer shawl, making his last prayer, raises his hands to heaven. A young girl is hanging from the balcony ready to jump to her death. German soldiers are shooting mercilessly.

I made the German soldiers faceless. Naturally the German soldiers had human faces, but in my painting, I could only see them without human expression. This is how I feel about them. On the ground, there are people who have been shot and a mother

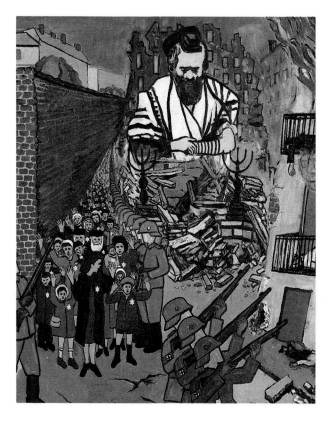

is protecting her baby from German bullets with her own body.

In the center of the painting, we see the ruins of the Warsaw Great Synagogue. Over the ruins is floating a figure of a Jewish man in prayer. This figure is taken from the photograph with the smiling soldiers. This is my tribute to this innocent victim of the Holocaust. His prayer symbolizes the unbroken continuity of the Jewish faith.

You will recognize the group of people, with the raised hands and the frightened little boy. Behind them is an endless number of people with raised hands. They are trapped between the wall and a long row of soldiers with machine guns and steel helmets. In the photograph we see the German soldiers in helmets, as they would fight on a battlefield against other soldiers.

My painting only shows a tiny part of the suffering of the Jews from the hands of the Germans.

Let us see what is going on on the Polish side of the wall.

It is clear from my painting that the unfortunate Jewish people were surrounded by a heartless, hostile world. Why did such hostility exist against the helpless Jewish minority?

Anti-Jewish feelings on religious grounds existed in Europe and Poland. When Hitler came to power, he set in motion intensive propaganda, consisting of lies and false accusations against the

Jews not as a religious group but as an inferior race.

According to Hitler's racial theories, people were not equal because of innate differences among human races. There were superior races, inferior races, the lowest races, and races of people who were not human at all. Naturally, according to Hitler and his followers, the Germans belonged to the super race, the master race. Slavs, the people of Eastern Europe, such as Poles, Russians and so on, belonged to the lower race, fit only to serve as slaves to the German masters. The lowest race, to which the Jews belonged, had to be killed. The black people, Hitler said, were not human beings at all. Most German and non-German people accepted Hitler's racial theories as long they were directed against the Jews.

My painting shows only the Warsaw Ghetto and the Polish people in Warsaw, but this is how it was in all the ghettos which the Germans established in Poland and in other parts of Europe.

In my painting you see people drinking and having fun. A huge clown, holding a bottle of vodka in one hand, is mocking the Jews. A merry-go-round is turning. Children are playing. These images are based on accounts given by survivors who witnessed similar scenes.

Another symbolic figure is that of a smiling priest. He represents the indifference of the Polish church to the tragedy which befell the Jews. The majority of Poles were very religious, but, unfortunately, the Polish Catholic Church did not call upon the Polish people to help the

Jews. It did not tell them how terrible it was to help the Germans to kill the Jews or to profit from Jewish misery. The Church kept silent. This silence encouraged the Germans to kill the Jews.

The Jewish people could not even expect help from the big powers, who were fighting the Germans. We see a balcony with three figures. They represent the United States, Great Britain and the Soviet Union. They are quietly looking on at what is happening in the Ghetto. Their indifference to the plight of the Jews is obvious. The great powers could easily have destroyed the death camps from the air or bombed the railroads leading to the camps. They could have let the world know by radio and newspapers what the Germans were doing to the Jews. Instead they kept silent.

However, in the sea of hatred and indifference surrounding the Jews, there were people who did help them and who saved Jewish lives. Those people, whom I call human angels, were like shining stars in the dark skies of Europe during the Nazi era. They helped Jewish people at the risk of their own lives, and many actually paid with their lives.

Such courageous human beings could be found among the Polish people in Warsaw, in other parts of Poland, and all over Europe. In Warsaw, a group of Poles formed an underground organization for helping Jews in hiding. In my painting, I pay tribute to those very few who helped to rescue Jewish lives. Under the "diplomats' " balcony, you can notice a couple separated from the crowd, turning their faces away in shame. The Jewish people will never forget the bravery and humanity of those members of the Polish clergy and the Catholic nuns who saved Jewish lives.

The Jews called these courageous and compassionate people Righteous Gentiles. Unfortunately, they were rare and few in number in comparison with those who expressed hostility toward the Holocaust victims.

THE JEWISH MOTHER IN THE GHETTO

Oil on canvas, 48″ × 70″ (110 cm. × 179 cm.), 1980

The central figure in this painting is a mother holding her child to protect it. Rifles are aimed at them by two figures in German helmets, who have swastikas on their arms, and blood-stained hands. I could not find a proper human expression that would match their inhuman acts, so I left them faceless. This scene is based on an actual photograph. The only difference is that in the photograph there is one soldier shooting at the mother and child. I met many people who witnessed similar scenes in ghettos and death camps.

In my painting, we see soldiers dragging the children from their mothers. We see where they are taking them—to be hurled into flames. Symbolically I show countless children in white shirts, like little innocent angels, with raised hands. In their midst there is a huge faceless German S.S. man with a machine gun. On his chest there is a monstrous iron cross. Hitler rewarded killers of children with medals and iron crosses.

Just as any mother in the world would have done, the Jewish mothers are either screaming, begging for mercy, or dying fighting

to protect their dearest ones. If we see one mother in my painting, we have to imagine countless numbers of them in similar situations.

In my painting I do not show a real Nazi oven—the crematorium in which they burned people. My oven is a German military helmet, turned upside down. In my imagination the German helmet was the inferno of Europe. Flames are bursting into the sky from the German helmet. They are red, mixed with human blood.

The flames are exploding into the heavens with a scream of a mother who is tearing her hair in agony. The shrieking voice of the mother is the voice of all Jewish mothers. It is the voice of all the murdered children. This piercing scream of despair is directed to the world. It asks, Civilization, where are you? Christian world, with all your teachings of love, where are you?

In my painting, two soldiers with swastikas on their arms, and helmets on their heads, are hurling live children into flames. Most of the world was watching in silence or looking the other way. You may ask: Is this possible? Aren't these images the pure imagination of an artist? I wish they were. Unfortunately, my images are only a slight shadow of the reality.

We see in my painting mothers running in panic with their children in their arms. They are rushing in all directions, desperate to find a hiding place. Soldiers with swastikas and helmets are following them with machine guns, looking for Jewish children. The oppressive Ghetto wall surrounds them. There is no escape. The walls of the red brick are made to seem still thicker by the pitiless hostility of the people who surround them.

On the other side of the wall, there are people who are busily using binoculars to observe life in the Jewish Ghetto. They do not

seem to feel disturbed. We see an elegantly dressed gentleman with white gloves. Maybe he is a professor or a dignitary. We also see a lady interested in taking a closer look at the people who are locked up in the Ghetto. Her hair is nicely done, she wears a beautiful dress, and has a cross around her neck. Through these people I represent our civilized world, of which a great part did nothing to stop the Holocaust.

No matter how unbearable and gloomy life was in the Ghetto, the Jews did not give up hope of survival and did not give up their faith. Underground we see the young mother feeding her baby, while her husband is preparing arms to resist the Germans. Another mother is rocking her baby to sleep. There is a mother observing the ritual of blessing her Sabbath candles.

In the painting *The Jewish Mother in the Ghetto*, I concentrated

the attention on the tragedy of the mother. My painting gives the impression that in the Ghetto there were only mothers with their children. In fact, the Ghetto was unbelievably crowded since the Germans did everything to make life there as miserable as possible. You can imagine the pain and suffering of the fathers, whose children were torn away to be killed.

The following painting is a tiny window for looking into a world of suffering inflicted on children only because they were born Jewish.

THE JEWISH CHILDREN IN GHETTOS
AND DEATH CAMPS

Oil on canvas, 70″ × 82″ (177.8 cm. × 208.3 cm.), 1981

A number of images in this painting are based on German photographs showing Jewish children in ghetto streets under the most deplorable conditions. After liberating the German death camps, the American army took pictures of Jewish children behind barbed wire.

You can easily find a relationship between my images and the photographs. Children are seen sleeping on the streets, some sitting helplessly, begging, abandoned and starving. Their parents must have been killed.

The two large figures of the little boy and girl with raised hands are of course taken from the photograph with the posing Nazi soldier who is aiming his machine gun at the child. The endless number of identical children symbolize the one and a half million youngsters murdered by Germans.

You may recognize the image of Anne Frank, whom I have framed symbolically in the ruins of a ghetto with all other Jewish children who perished. She is one of many victims. I took her image from one of the photographs saved after her arrest.

By introducing Anne Frank into my painting I emphasize that her diary is also the story of many Jewish children. I pay tribute to her memory. Luckily we know her from her writing. Many thousands of young people like Anne Frank perished in the German inferno without leaving a trace of what they had to say.

In the left side of the painting, I depicted children being loaded into the cattle trains. The photograph on the next page was probably taken by an S.S. man. In it we see children marching to the train, with yellow stars on their coats. The Germans, after occupying a country, issued an order that a Jewish person of any age had to wear a yellow star. The punishment for breaking this rule was death.

In my painting all the children wear yellow stars. The cattle car is packed to capacity with the little children ready to go on their last journey. The huge German S.S. man is there holding his gun ready against the children.

Numberless cattle cars are rolling from all over Europe to the death camp. They are filled with Jewish children.

Over the entrance to the camp, the Germans put a big sign written in German: *"Arbeit Macht Frei."* It meant "Work Will Make You Free." The sign was intended to fool people. It was a place not for work, but for being killed. In my painting I show in a symbolic way what the camp behind the gates and barbed wire meant. The whole ground is shooting with flames, the flames of the Holocaust. German helmets explode with fire.

The meaning of the German eagle, the swastika on its heart, dripping with blood, is clear.

From both sides of my painting, from behind

the Ghetto wall and barbed wires, and behind the flames of the death camp and the German eagle, we see hands. They represent the millions of hands saluting Hitler. We see beautifully groomed hands, manicured, some in white gloves. These are hands of a civilized world saluting the acts of a barbarian world.

By showing these saluting hands, I wanted to suggest that Hitler and the Nazis, because of their intense anti-Jewish propaganda, had the support of the majority of the German people and of a great part of the people of Europe. The Germans carried out the annihilation of the Jews in full view of the local population, but the people kept silent. The great powers did not make any effort to inform the world about the Nazi crimes against the Jews. The Holocaust came about because the people of Europe were like Cain of the Bible—they were not their brother's keeper.

The long cattle trains packed with Jews ran through the fields and countrysides of Europe. I have included a Christian church and a road cross. The starving and dying Jews in the trains could not expect help from anyone.

Auschwitz

The real death camps didn't look like my painting. The Germans were well organized. Each death camp had many hundreds of specially built barracks and buildings for tens of thousands of prisoners. To kill and burn them, the Germans installed gas chambers and crematories. The S.S. soldiers lived in nice buildings with gardens and flowers. For years, trains brought there daily tens of thousands of Jewish people from all over Europe.

Among the endless numbers of cattle trains, rolling day and night, carrying Jewish children, we have to include the one hundred thousand children from the Warsaw Ghetto. Among the tragic deportees were also the children of the orphanage run by the famous Dr. Janusz Korczak (*Yanoosh Kortshak*).

His real name was Henryk Goldszmidt. He was a medical doctor, a world-famous educator, and director of a Jewish orphanage. He used the name Dr. Janusz Korczak as an author of children's books,

Dr. Janusz Korczak

which were translated from Polish into many European languages. Dr. Korczak distinguished himself by his devotion and love for children. He especially showed great dedication to orphans.

When the Germans invaded Warsaw, Dr. Korczak had to move his Jewish orphanage into the Ghetto. In August 1942, when the S.S. started to deport all the children from the Ghetto, they ordered Dr. Korczak to prepare his 200 orphans to march to the train station. The Germans told Dr. Korczak he could remain home. He refused to abandon his children at a time of despair and walked with them into the cattle train. He was murdered together with his children in the death camp Treblinka. Dr. Janusz Korczak will be remembered as a great humanitarian, whose life was a legend of selflessness and devotion to mankind.

On the upper right side of the painting we see barbed wires, and behind them imprisoned children in camp uniforms, like criminals, and an old lady with two youngsters walking to their deaths. These heartbreaking scenes are based on actual photographs.

Also based on a photograph is the group of children, like living skeletons. I included faceless, dummy-like figures of German doctors with swastikas on their arms. They are looking into huge test tubes filled with blood. This symbolizes the Nazi obsession with the racial qualities of human blood. Many German doctors collaborated with the Nazis and helped them in their program of killing the Jews. They treated the Jews as nonhumans and carried out all kinds of medical experiments on them, as if they were animals. We see in my painting books and microscopes. This is to show that the German doctors were serious about their racial theories.

After the war, independent scientists and doctors proved that all the Nazi racial theories were false. They agreed that it is not true that different races of people have blood of different quality. Contrary to the Nazi racial theories, it was proven that by nature all people are equal.

Let us now return inside the walls of the Ghetto. As you know, the purpose of the wall was to seal off the Jews and to destroy them by starvation. But the Jewish people resisted by smuggling food into the Ghetto. In this struggle for survival, children took a very active part. Risking their lives, they climbed walls, sneaked through crowds, or crawled through openings to buy food for their parents on the Polish side. The punishment for smuggling was very severe, often death. In my

painting the young smuggler is running in terror, carrying food on his back. Young people smuggled not only food but weapons for the forthcoming armed resistance against the Germans.

The Germans gave strict orders forbidding any schools or the teaching of children. In spite of this, there were Jewish schools in bunkers and hideouts. The Jewish people made the greatest effort to continue their normal life as much as possible. In the Ghetto it was an important form of resistance.

In my painting you see a school with teachers and children in the underground. A mother is hugging her baby in the hope of survival. Children are hiding weapons.

The next painting is devoted to the most important and most heroic event in Jewish recent history and in the history of anti-Nazi resistance in Europe.

THE WARSAW GHETTO UPRISING—
HEROISM AND RESISTANCE

Oil on canvas, 62" × 144" (148 cm. × 366 cm.), 1982

One thousand years ago the Jewish people established the first settlement in Poland. Warsaw, its capital, became the greatest center of Jewish cultural and spiritual life in the world. On May 16, 1943, the German General Jürgen Stroop reported to his superior that no more Jews existed in Warsaw. The first painting, *Warsaw Ghetto Streets 1943*, shows the wasteland that Stroop made of the Warsaw Ghetto, an area which once had the largest and most thriving Jewish community.

This painting depicts the courage, the unbelievable heroism, and vitality of the Jewish people who rose up in revolt against their German oppressors. To the amazement of the whole world, the mighty German army had to fight for five weeks to overcome this rebellion which is known as the Warsaw Ghetto Uprising.

The resistance was organized by the twenty-one-year-old Morde-chai Anielewicz, (*Mordekay Anielevitsh*) with a small band of followers. Despite general starvation and the dangerous conditions in the Ghetto, they made a superhuman effort to find arms. Their

Polish neighbors, who had a well-organized underground army of resistance, refused to help the Jews or to sell them armaments. It was almost an impossible mission for the young Jewish fighters to find weapons, but in spite of all odds, the Jewish fighters did not give up. They bought handguns, a limited number of rifles and a few machine guns. Most of the weapons, such as gasoline bottles and bombs, they made themselves.

In 1943, Anielewicz had about seven hundred young men and women ready to fight, with inadequate guns and ammunition. The Germans had an army of thousands of soldiers equipped with tanks, armored cars, airplanes and artillery.

The Germans chose April 19, 1943, the first day of the Jewish Holiday of Passover, to start their final destruction of the Ghetto and the deportation of the remaining Jews. Cattle trains were waiting on the tracks. The S.S. troops, along with Polish police and Ukrainian volunteers, surrounded the Ghetto walls with heavy weapons.

The Germans were sure of a quick victory. They expected that after two days, not one Jew would be left alive. The Jewish fighters were poorly armed but high in courage. They were inspired by the Passover Holiday and remembering the liberation of their ancestors from Egyptian bondage, were ready to fight against the new slavery. When the Germans moved into the Ghetto they were met with such gunfire that they had to retreat with their tanks and armored cars, leaving behind many dead and wounded. The S.S. men and the heavily armed German troops ran for cover shouting: "The Jews are shooting," surprised that the "subhuman" Jews fought back so vigorously.

For the young Jewish fighters, it was not a question of victory over the German army. They knew this was impossible. What they wanted was to prove to the arrogant Germans that the Jews could fight and defend their human dignity and the honor of their people. After a few days General Stroop found that he was suffering too many losses. Since he could not overcome the heroic Ghetto fighters in open street fightings, he decided to set the whole Ghetto on fire and to blow up building after building with people inside. He knew that Jews were hidden in underground bunkers, so he ordered his troops to inject poison gas into the hideouts to chase them out. Stroop ordered his soldiers to use special flamethrowers and to drop bombs from airplanes over the Ghetto.

The photograph shows General Stroop on a Warsaw Ghetto street. Soldiers on his staff are happily smiling at the camera. Stroop is also posing but is busy looking at the burning buildings.

My painting gives only a slight idea of the inferno in which the Jewish people found themselves. As in other paintings, I present symbolic images of the German army. This time they are in the form of monstrous barrels of tanks directed against the Ghetto. The tanks which you see are not real. They are, rather, monster machines in which the German helmets, with metallic faces, form one piece which is spreading destruction. The human and machine are one frightening unit. They all have swastikas and black crosses, which show that they are German death machines. You see them on the ground and in the air.

The whole Ghetto is engulfed in flames. In front you see parts of crumbling walls with balconies, windows and cracks. Young fighters are shooting with guns and rifles or throwing bottles of gasoline. The walls are falling apart. At any moment the fighters will die under the ruins. But they continue fighting.

In the very center of the painting you see in large scale a group of fighters. Three strong hands are holding a pole with a flag of Zion. It is the Jewish flag of hope with inspiring words written in blood in Hebrew and Yiddish: "Long Live the Jewish People." Young rebels are shooting with handguns at the enemy machines. One fighter is ripping apart the hated Nazi flag as he dies. A young boy is delivering bottles of gasoline to the woman fighter.

On the right side of the group is a young boy throwing a lighted bottle into the Nazi machine. Many heroic children took part in the armed uprising. We shall always remember them.

Among the group of fighters is another figure holding a holy scroll (Torah) tightly in one hand. The man is covered with a prayer shawl. He is raising his other hand high into the heaven in a desperate last prayer. Even though he is dying, he still has his Torah, his faith in God, Judaism, and humanity.

In order to escape the Germans the Jews dug deeply underground, creating a system of hundreds of bunkers and tunnels. A similar network of passages was built through roofs and attics.

The headquarters of the Ghetto Uprising was located in a well-prepared bunker on Mila Street, number 18. From there Mordechai Anielewicz and his staff organized their daring operations against the Germans.

One day the S.S., using the most sophisticated instruments and special dogs, discovered the bunker Mila 18. Anielewicz and his

Mordecai Anielewicz,
painted by Israel Bernbaum

Dr. Emmanuel Ringelblum

comrades refused to give themselves up. The Germans threw gas bombs into the bunker. When they could not find any other way out, the young Mordechai, with about one hundred of his fellow resistance fighters, committed suicide. Unfortunately, it was too late for most of the young heroes when a hidden exit in the bunker was found. Only twenty-one fighters escaped. Among them was the courageous Zywia Lubetkin. She was one of the very few who survived the war to bear witness to the terrible drama of the bunker of Mila 18 and of the Warsaw Ghetto Uprising.

Zywia Lubetkin was one of the closest collaborators of Mordechai Anielewicz, and praised him as a noble human being. Mordechai Anielewicz died at the age of twenty-three. The central figure in my painting, the hero with the flag, shooting, is my tribute to the commander in chief of the Warsaw Ghetto Uprising, Mordechai Anielewicz.

Another man of great character and unusual courage and dedication was Dr. Emmanuel Ringelblum. We see his image, sitting and writing in a bunker. He was an historian. While in mortal danger, he gathered for his archives material about the life of the Jews in the Ghetto. After the war the so-called Ringelblum Archives were recovered. They serve now as the most important source of information on life in the Warsaw Ghetto.

Below Dr. Ringelblum's bunker, you see in my painting men, women and children running through tunnels seeking safety. One man is anxious to save a holy scroll, a Torah. A fighter is standing ready to protect his people.

The will to survive was always strong among the Ghetto people. In their desperate attempt to avoid deportation, they tried to escape through the sewers to the Polish side where they hoped to find a hideout or to reach the partisans in the forests. You see them, in my painting, walking immersed in sewage water to their shoulders. Some are holding children on their backs.

Below you see a Ghetto underground "factory" of homemade weapons. Ghetto fighters are moving through tunnels armed mostly with bottles filled with gasoline.

There is a cave under the ruins of a building where a mother, still hoping for survival, is hugging and protecting her children.

On the upper part of my painting is a building (see detail on page 56). On one side it is bursting into flames, but on the other side, a Passover celebration is taking place. The people of the Ghetto, even under the enemy's fire, did not give up celebrating the holiday which glorified freedom for the Jews and freedom for mankind delivered from slavery and tyranny. It was an act of immense heroism to celebrate Passover under such conditions.

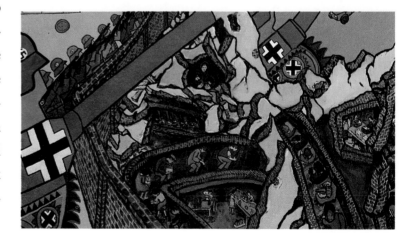

In another building with a damaged roof, you see people looking for escape and fighters seeking positions from which to battle the enemy. The blue-and-white flag, which is the symbol of hope, announces the resistance.

A column of German ambulances with red crosses is moving from the battlefields with their dead and injured.

There are walls on each side. Inside the walls is a sea of fire, death and destruction. Outside the walls people are enjoying an interesting spectacle (shown on page 57). Some are soaring high into the sky on a merry-go-round. As usual my images present events symbolically, telling not only about the indifference but also about the rejoicing of the Polish people, oblivious to the Jews dying in the flames of the Ghetto.

Survivors reported this many times. The great Polish writer and poet Czeslaw Milosz wrote a poem in 1943. He was deeply disturbed at seeing happy people riding on merry-go-rounds next to the walls of the burning Warsaw Ghetto. In his poem *"Campo di Fiory"* he describes how the young Polish couples were wildly spinning into the blue sky under the blaring dance music which was drowned by the salvos of bursting bombs behind the Ghetto. Mr. Milosz received the Nobel Prize for Literature in 1980.

Fortunately, Czeslaw Milosz was not totally alone in his human nobility. There were other courageous Poles who helped their Jewish friends. It is important not to forget them.

In this painting I again pay tribute to those unsung heroes through the image of the building with the uncovered attic, showing Jewish people in hiding. A man is delivering food to them through a secret opening in the ceiling, while a woman watches at the window to see if a stranger is in sight. This couple are Polish Christians. You see a cross on their wall. These people symbolize human goodness, compassion, and belief in humanity. The number of these Poles was not great but they must never be forgotten. They were their brother's keeper.

Here again you see the ruins of the Warsaw Great Synagogue with upright menorahs. They symbolize hope and promise for the survival of the Jewish people.

At the ruins of the Synagogue you see the Ghetto wall transformed into endless cattle trains. On the horizon you see the fire and smoke of the death camps. In the train station are the piles of luggage which the Germans had forced the Jewish victims to leave behind so they could steal them.

A handful of Jewish survivors, from the destroyed Ghetto, managed to reach the forests. There they joined partisans fighting the

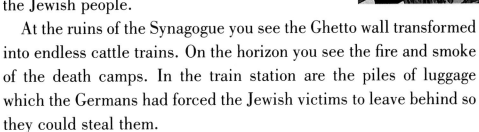

Germans or they formed their own groups. In my painting a truck with Jewish escapees is approaching the woods. The small group of Jewish partisans is the symbol of all Jewish fighters and partisans in Poland, Russia, and everywhere else in Europe.

The blue sky and the green forests in my painting symbolize new hopes and new expectations for a world of freedom, equality and justice for all.

It took almost six years to liberate Europe from the Nazi nightmare, but finally Hitler was defeated. It was a result of a great effort and enormous sacrifices on the part of the people of Europe, the United States, Great Britain, the Soviet Union, Canada, and of other parts of the world.

Jewish people died in the Holocaust. Many of them, as I showed in my paintings, died resisting the enemy. Some gave strong spiritual resistance, defying the Germans' inhumanity. Some fought the Germans with arms. The Jewish people played a great part in combatting Hitler's armies. One and a half million Jewish men and women fought in American, British, Soviet, Canadian, Australian and other armies on all battlegrounds of Europe and Africa. Many died and many distinguished themselves by their bravery.

Fifty thousand Jewish partisans fought the Germans in the forests of Poland, Russia and Western Europe. The Warsaw Ghetto Uprising, although exceptional in its significance and extent, was one of many revolts in ghettos and death camps.

In April 1945, World War II was at its end. The survivors of the camps were liberated. Human skeletons, wearing no more than torn rags, were set free to start life again. Most of them were left sole survivors of large families. Their homes in their native countries had been destroyed or taken over by strangers or by their non-Jewish neighbors. The Jewish survivors found themselves isolated, again confronting unfriendliness and even hostility. Some were threatened and chased from their own homes. Once more they had to escape and to look for a new home.

Fortunately, the nations of the world recognized the great sacrifices which the Jewish people had made, and accepted the establishment of a Jewish State. The centuries' long dream of the Jewish people, of a homeland, in the land of their ancestors, served as a foundation for the new State of Israel. The ashes of the Holocaust, the heroism of the Jewish people, and their unbroken will to live and to build a new life made it possible.

In 1948, Israel was proclaimed an independent Jewish State. The United States, through its President, Harry S Truman, was the first nation to recognize Israel. Shortly thereafter Israel became a full member of the United Nations.

Israel was the only place in the world which opened its arms to the survivors of the Holocaust, receiving them as free people in their own country. Those who miraculously escaped death in the Holocaust found a home where they have since built their new life and a permanent future.

The Jewish people who suffered so much from injustice and persecutions, tyrants and dictators have built their country, the State of Israel, on the basis of democracy, freedom and human rights for all. These were the visions and ideals of those who fought and died in the ruins of the ghettos.

To prevent the tragic past from being forgotten, the people of Israel established a great Holocaust Center and museum in Jerusalem, called Yad-Vashem (Remembrance Authority). People from all over the world come to see it and to learn a great lesson of the past.

The surviving Ghetto fighters established their own kibbutz in Israel, not far from Haifa, with another museum of the Holocaust, called Beit Lahomei Haghetaot (the Museum of the Ghetto Fighters).

The Jewish people did not forget the courageous Righteous Gentiles. They have built an Alley of Righteous Gentiles in Jerusalem in gratitude and tribute to those who at the risk of their own lives helped Jews to survive.

It is important to know that in the German system of death camps the Nazis also murdered five million non-Jews. The total number of victims of Nazi atrocities was eleven million. The Jews were killed because of the German special program which they called "The Final Solution of the Jewish Problem" and we call the Holocaust; the non-Jews were killed because they opposed the Nazi rule.

It is also important to mention that Hitler and his Nazi followers, in their obsession with superior racial human qualities, ordered all handicapped and disabled people, German and foreign, to be killed.

The Germans nurtured a particular hatred against the Poles.

Over two and a half million were killed. Many hundreds of thousands were sent to Germany for slave labor. Over two hundred thousand young Polish children were kidnapped to Germany, because the Germans found them "racially valuable" and wanted to bring them up as good Nazi Germans. Hitler gave instructions for the complete destruction of the Polish culture and economy.

The people of occupied Russia and other parts of Europe met no better fate. Their countries were turned into wasteland and the people into slaves. Historians are of the opinion that the destruction of the Jews was intended to be only the first step in a gigantic program of Germanization of the whole world. A more frightful and darker world is hard to imagine.

The Jews were singled out first by Hitler because they would be the easiest target for a program of mass destruction. As you learned from my paintings, the majority of people did not much care about the fate of the Jews. Some even helped the Germans in the plan for their destruction. Hatred for the Jews made the people blind and they failed to see that they themselves could be the next victims. Hitler was not only anti-Semitic, but openly anti-Christian. He promised that at the right time, he would destroy Christianity as a religion. Had Hitler not been defeated, Christianity would have shared the same fate as Judaism. There were no limits to his destructive ideas.

From children's letters I assume that classes discussed with the teacher what should be done to prevent such a tragedy as the Holocaust from occuring again. As our country is democratic, so is the American school. All children regardless of racial, religious or ethnic background are entitled to be treated with equal care and love.

In Germany, before Hitler became Chancellor, Jewish children were treated equally with all German children. However, after Hitler and his Nazi Party had taken over power, the Jewish children were abused, excluded from German schools because of their "inferior" race.

The Nazis introduced a strict military discipline into the schools. Children were taught racial theories of the supremacy of the German race and the inferiority of all the other people and especially of the Jews. They learned about the greatness of their new leader, Adolf Hitler, and about the great German empire that was to dominate the world.

The young German generation was brought up in a spirit of

militarism, racism, prejudice and hatred of everything which was not German. The result of such education was World War II and the Holocaust.

We ask again: How can we prevent such catastrophic events from recurring? The answer may be found in ourselves. We must reject all racial theories about differences of human qualities among people as false, inhuman and immoral. We must not prejudge people because of the color of their skin, religion or origin. Instead, we must practice the principle of absolute equality and justice for all. We must learn to be tolerant and accept differences among people. Instead of erecting walls and fences separating human beings from each other, we will open gates of mutual understanding and open our hearts for mutual respect. Instead of hating we will listen and learn from each other.

May no children of any nation suffer again from such tragedy as the Holocaust. A Holocaust can never take place in a world where love and brotherhood among people prevail. Never can a Holocaust occur in a world where human dignity is respected and human life is sacred.

Contrary to what happened during the Holocaust we must feel pain when our fellow man is hurt. We must not remain indifferent when others suffer.

We learned why the Jewish children were murdered. Their deaths will not be in vain when all children of all nations will join hands in brotherhood and love and will solemnly declare to the world of today and of all tomorrows: I am my brother's keeper.

Bor, Josef. *The Terezin Requiem*. New York: Avon, 1978.

Dobroszycki, Lucjan, and Barbara Kirshenblatt-Gimblett. *Image Before My Eyes: A Photographic History of Jewish Life in Poland 1864–1939*. New York: Schocken, 1977.

Eisenberg, Azriel, Editor. *The Lost Generation: Children in the Holocaust*. New York: Pilgrim Press, 1982.

The Diary of Eva Heyman. Jerusalem: Yad Vashem, 1974.

Flinker, Moshe. *Young Moshe's Diary*. New York: Board of Jewish Education, 1971.

Frank, Anne. *Diary of a Young Girl*. New York: Pocket Books, 1971.

Katz, William Loren. *An Album of Nazism*. New York: Franklin Watts, 1979.

Meltzer, Milton. *Never to Forget*. New York: Harper and Row, 1976.

Noar, Gertrude. *The Third Reich in Perspective*. New York: Anti-Defamation League of B'nai B'rith, 1961.

Richter, Hans Peter. *Friedrich*. New York: Dell, 1973.

Rossel, Seymour. *The Holocaust*. New York: Franklin Watts, 1981.

Rubin, Arnold P. *The Evil That Men Do*. New York: Messner, 1977.

Shirer, William L. *The Rise & Fall of Adolf Hitler*. New York: Random House, 1963.

Szajkowski, Soza. *An Illustrated Sourcebook on the Holocaust*. New York: Ktav.

Volavkova, H., ed. *I Never Saw Another Butterfly*. New York: McGraw Hill, 1964.

Wiesenthal, Simon. *The Sunflower*. New York: Schocken, 1977.